BEAUTIFUL
SCOTLAND
W. H. Murray

Scotland is considered by many to be the
most beautiful country in the world. Just
why, can be seen from the outstanding
photographs reproduced in this book –
over half of them in full colour. These
provide a dazzling pictorial record of the
very best of Scotland's varied scenery, as
well as her architecture and pageantry:
Loch Lomond, Glencoe and Rannoch
Moor: Skye and the imposing grandeur
of the far north: St Andrews and the
fishing village of Crail; abbeys, country
houses and castles such as Melrose,
Abbotsford, Holyroodhouse, and
Inverary; the Edinburgh Tattoo and the
Highland Games.

    W. H. Murray, a Scot who lives at Loch
Goil in Argyllshire, has written an
introduction that is both informative and
evocative. Together, text and pictures,
provide a souvenir of Scotland's
incomparable beauty that will be
treasured by fellow Scotsmen and visitors
alike.

overleaf Eilean Donan Castle, Loch Alsh,
Kintail

BEAUTIFUL SCOTLAND

W. H. Murray

B. T. BATSFORD LTD., London

First published 1976
Reprinted 1978
© B. T. Batsford Ltd., 1976
ISBN 0 7134 3217 9

Printed by
Leefung-Asco Printers Ltd.,
Hong Kong
for the publishers
B. T. Batsford Ltd.
4 Fitzhardinge Street, London W I Ho AH

CONTENTS

Falls of Dochart, Killin, Perthshire

During the last 40 years, I have had the good fortune to travel through some 20-odd countries between Britain and Tibet. Vivid as that experience has been, it has long since brought me to a conclusion wholly unexpected when I first set out – that the most varied beauties of landscape, the most brilliant colour, the finest subtleties of light and shade, are to be found not at the ends of the earth, but on our own doorstep in Scotland.

The great varieties of landscape are caused by an equal variety in the underlying rock, and by crustal movements, which lifting some parts and depressing others have given Scotland four main divisions of structure – the Highlands, Lowlands, Southern Uplands, and to the west a barrier fringe of 550 islands. The rocks have been forming and re-forming over the last 3000 million years; they have been raised to Alpine heights and eroded by weather to sea-level. The most recent elevation occurred only some 25 million years ago, when Scotland (then a part of Scandinavia) was raised up as a high tableland, which extended far beyond its present bounds to the continental shelf 20 miles west of St Kilda. Rain and rivers carved this plateau into the mountains and glens of the Highlands, and into the broader valleys and gentler slopes of the Southern Uplands. Between the two, a great subsidence nearly 50 miles wide formed the rift valley of the Central Lowlands. The Highlands to their north were thus given a clearly marked base line running from Arran on the Firth of Clyde to Stonehaven on the east coast. This geological fault-line, known as the 'Highland Line', is still subject to earth tremors, notably around Crieff at its centre.

Between 10 and 15 million years ago, the Atlantic seaboard of Europe subsided. The forested plain linking Scotland to Norway was submerged under the North Sea, while the Atlantic flooded into the Highlands' westward-running glens, filled the valley of the Minch, and isolated the western hill-tops as islands. A wildly serrated coast-line was thus created, with deep sea-lochs or fiords running 30 and 40 miles into the mountains, and a host of islands later called the Hebrides – most likely from the Norse word *Havbredey*, 'The Isles on the Edge of the Sea'. All was further shaped by Ice Age glaciers that later poured off the Highland ice-cap.

By the time Scotland received its first-known men around 6000 BC in the Boreal period, the land was covered in primeval forest, mainly oak, birch, hazel, and Scots pine. And that would be the state of the land today were it not for man's fires and fellings, which have shorn the Lowlands of almost all its tree cover and reduced the Highland forest to a fraction of its old strength. Scotland today has 7.7 million hectares of land, of which 0.8 million are woodland and 0.4 million mainly urban. The remaining 6.5 million are in agricultural use, mainly rough grazing, for only one quarter is under crops and grass. The brilliant seasonal colour-changes in vegetation are caused by the Atlantic atmosphere and northern latitude.

THE LOWLANDS

In broad, general terms, the Lowlands are gently rolling country divided by half-a-dozen hill groups into narrower plains. Drained by the rivers Forth, Clyde, Tay, and Esk, the plains are covered in glacial boulder-clay, which preserved the underlying coal-fields and ironstone. That made possible the heavy industrial development of Strathclyde, where Glasgow, already prosperous from the tobacco trade with America, turned to shipbuilding in the nineteenth century. Three-fifths of Scotland's population live in the central Lowlands. Its natural beauty has been largely laid waste in consequence, but south-west of Glasgow the pasturelands of Ayrshire remain almost intact.

Glasgow is always worth visiting, not only for a few fine buildings, like the twelfth-century cathedral, Provand's Lordship, and the School of Art (by Rennie Mackintosh), or for the Art Gallery at Kelvingrove (the best outside London), but for its convenience as a base from which to explore the wooded dairylands of Ayrshire, the Burns Country around Alloway, Culzean Castle, and still further south, the Galloway Hills between Ayr and the Solway Firth.

THE BORDERS

The Southern Uplands stretch 100 miles west to east in seven hill group – the Galloways, the Lowther Hills, Ettrick Forest, the Lammermuir Hills and their northern offshoots the Moorfoots and Pentlands, and, to south of all, the Cheviots. Their clean open grasslands rise above 2000 feet, often criss-crossed below by dry-stone dykes, sometimes wooded lightly by native trees, or heavily planted in spruce. They carry more sheep to the square mile than any other part of Scotland.

The Galloway Hills, on their south or Dumfriessshire side above the Solway, have rich farmland by Annandale and Nithsdale. Narrow lanes penetrate deep countryside, where the hedgerows are thick with blossom. Cornfields spread wide to either side, while the open, higher ground is alive with larks, peewits, and snipe. Farther east lie the Borders proper – the shires of Roxburgh and Berwick along the Border itself, with Selkirk and Peebles to their north traditionally included. The English side of the Border is rough moorland, but the Scots side spreads out in wooded valleys and rolling dales threaded by slow rivers.

The exploration of the Borders is best done from Edinburgh, or from one of the Border towns such as Kelso, Jedburgh, Peebles, Selkirk, Melrose, Galashiels, and Hawick. The land is not only beautiful in itself, with its contrast of bare upland grazing with well-sheltered dales, but it also bears a wealth of architectural masterpiece and spectacle in ruined castles and abbeys. Other ancient stone buildings and bridges abound. The landscape seems more peaceful than any other well-inhabited countryside of Scotland, but the many towns are fully alive. They hold to their traditional woollen industries, notable tweed weaving, and other light industries have been moving in.

In no other part of Scotland has so much good work in stone been built up only to be destroyed. Border history has been savage, and the vengeance exacted by English armies ruthless. The most famous examples of medieval architecture of which there are substantial remains are the abbeys at Jedburgh, Dryburgh, Kelso, and Melrose. Melrose, first founded on the banks of the Tweed as a Cistercian monastery in 1136, has been several times destroyed (by Edward II and Richard II among other army commanders) but always rebuilt. The Perpendicular style now predominates. The rich window traceries in red sandstone are notable works of art, the most famous being the five-light south window. The heart of Robert the Bruce is buried under the chancel's east window. The Abbey is described in several of Sir Walter Scott's books (*The Abbot*, *The Monastery*, and the *Lay of the Last Minstrel*) – and not surprisingly, since his own house of Abbotsford (open to the public) stands less than three miles west. He built his house on the Tweed as a baronial mansion, but his favourite view was from Bemersyde east of Melrose, looking to the Eildon Hills. The Eildon's were the scene of that great Border ballad, in which the Queen of Elfland met Thomas the Rhymer and led him into seven years' captivity, from which he returned with a tongue that could speak only truth.

> And see ye not yon bonnie road
> That winds about the fernie brae?
> That is the road to fair Elfland
> Where thou and I this night maun gae.

The most interesting house on the Tweed is Traquair in Peebleshire, 10 miles west of Abbotsford. It is Scotland's oldest inhabited mansion. William the Lion lived there around 1209, since when it has been used by 26 other Scottish or English kings. One surviving tower is a thousand years old, but the main block dates from 1642.

EDINBURGH

Edinburgh, whether visited before or after the Border country, will appear a worthy capital. Its two soubriqets, Auld Reekie and the Modern Athens, sum up the character of its two main parts, the Old Town and the New Town. Except on the north side, which overlooks the Firth of Forth, the city is ringed by hills. The Old Town is built on a steep rocky ridge running east to west. On the highest eastern crest, the castle stands guard over all. There was a fort here from prehistoric times, but the oldest surviving buildings, Queen Margaret's chapel and King David's tower (the ancient keep), date from the eleventh and early twelfth centuries. The ridge slopes down one mile to flat ground below Arthur's Seat, and here on the flats of King's Park Holyrood Palace was first built in 1501, and rebuilt in 1670 for Charles II. The old town grew naturally on the 'Royal Mile' of the ridge between castle and palace, for the one was the source of power

and protection, the other of court authority. Between were St Giles Church, the Parliament Hall, and others. Since the ridge was narrow, the burghers' houses, together with those of the nobles, gentlemen, professional men, and tradesmen, were crowded close in tall tenements with common yards and stairways, yet with individual varieties in height and the design of crow-stepped gables, corbels, turrets, and of harled wall-surfacings. A good example is White Horse Close, from which stage coaches departed from the Canongate for London. Having neither space nor drainage, the whole became a *beau-monde* slum. Slops were thrown out of windows on to the steep narrow streets with the warning cry of 'Gardyloo!' (*Guardez l'eau*). Granted modern plumbing and maintenance, the scene today along the Royal Mile retains only a little of its old character, for two-thirds of the high tenements have been removed.

The New Town to the north, created from 1767, is Scotland's finest urban landscape. The North Loch below the castle ridge was drained – it is now the site of Princes Street gardens – then on the far side, where cattle grazed, handsome public buildings and family houses were built in sandstone, laid out spaciously in classical squares and circuses. The Georgian style was best exemplified by Robert Adam. Three of his finest constructions were Register House in Princes Street close to Calton Hill, the north side of Charlotte Square, and the University's Old Quad. Calton Hill gives a bird's eye view of the city's main features – the New Town stretching down to the shore and to the Port of Leith; to the left, the Old Town along the castle rock; and between, the valley of the Nor' Loch, now occupied by gardens, the railway, and Princes Street.

EAST LOWLANDS

North across the Forth, the East Lowlands spread through the Fife peninsula and up the coast through Perth and Angus to Aberdeen, then on by the Moray Firth to Caithness. These lowlands have a North Sea atmosphere wholly different from the Atlantic coast and Borders. This is drier, sharper country with a brisker air. Its people have a drier tongue and wit. Up and down the coast to either side of Stonehaven, where the Highland Line meets the sea, are numerous fishing villages with stone-walled harbours, but none can equal those of Fife between the Tay and Forth, several of which, like Crail and Culross, have become living museums of vernacular architecture. Fife offers a wealth of opportunity for explorations into man's history, and St Andrews is the ideal centre. The university (1412) is Scotland's oldest. The colour plate shows the old stone pier with the twelfth-century tower of St Regulus' Church rising behind – the main surviving fragment of the surrounding cathedral buildings, which were demolished at the Reformation.

An eye-catching feature of the coastal royal burghs is their sixteenth- and seventeenth-century houses with crow-stepped gables and red or orange pantiled roofs. These have striking effect when seen above the harbour wall at Crail. Culross near the Forth estuary adds to such typical features outer stairways to the first storeys and ogee spires. This former coal-mining and salt-panning town has been rescued from dereliction by the National Trust for Scotland, whose restorations have extended to 'little houses' all along the Fife coast, and made of them a comprehensive exhibition of seventeenth-century domestic life.

THE HEBRIDES

Scotland has no greater scenic contrast than that between her east and west seaboards: the one a smooth lowland coast, the other wildly fretted and mountainous, screened to seaward by two archipelagos, the Inner and Outer Hebrides. They comprise 550 islands, of which only 64 are inhabited. The Inner Hebrides lie close in to the coast in a double rank 142 miles long. Skye and Mull are the biggest, and by sea the most quickly accessible. The Outer Isles, 35 to 50 miles from the mainland, form a compact line 130 miles long, often called the Long Isle, of which the biggest are Lewis, Harris, and the Uists. All inhabited groups have sea- and air-ferry services from the mainland.

The isles take every shape from pancakes to spires. Seen across the broad channel of the Minch, the Outer Isles undulate along the horizon like a low hill-spine, lilac-coloured or black against the changing sky. The crest rises twice to around 2000 feet, and is formed of Scotland's oldest rock, Lewisian gneiss, radiometrically dated to 2,600 million years. A close approach to their east coasts can be daunting. The glaciers that once ground across their backs have stripped off the soil, leaving bare rock on which only a thin cover of heather has been able to lodge. But the western shores are fair to the eye. More gently curved, they slope to shallower water, where huge seas have spread the beaches with white shell-sand. The cliffs between bays are noisy with sea-birds. Behind the beaches lie the machairs – sandy grasslands covered all summer long with wild flowers, and grazed by cattle. Between these contrasting coasts rise brown moorlands, where green fields are either tucked in the hollows or stretch like aprons from crofting townships to the sea. Flowers grow thick by ditch and stream. Down the long length of the moorlands stretch a multitude of freshwater lochs, some ringed by waterlilies and all alive with duck, or greylag geese, or trout.

Croft houses have been modernised. Thatched roofs are rare in the Inner Isles, but are still often seen in the Outer. The old black houses, built in drystone with double walls, no chimneys, and the thatch set on the inner walls to deprive the gale-winds of purchase (and to give easy access for repairs), are now rarely occupied in Lewis except as weaving sheds. They are still lived in at some out of the way spots like Valtos on Loch Roag, or in small islands like Berneray and Eriskay, where they have been modernised by the addition of chimneys, wood panelling, and floor-boards. They fit perfectly into the island scene. In the gale-stricken winter months they are warmer and more comfortable than modern houses.

The Inner Hebrides are of different character. They are widely scattered, much more heavily bayed, and for the most part stand high out of the water – especially Skye, Rum, and Mull. The difference is caused by the change in rock, which here is volcanic. Being softer and more brittle than gneiss, the lavas have been hugely eroded. The greater land-heights and hills give better shelter for trees and the taller-growing flowers. The basalt of Mull and Skye breaks down to good soil. Therefore Skye is heavily crofted and bare of trees except at plantations; the grass is lush compared to the Outer Isles. The Inner Isles pay for such privileges with a heavier rainfall drawn down by the higher hills.

Skye is crowned by the Cuillin. Twenty rock peaks at the south end encircle Loch Coruisk to a height of 3,200 feet. The mountain scene is unique in Britain, for the rock is naked gabbro and the peaks linked by a continuous ridge, whose flanks have been deeply gouged by glaciers. The traverse along the tops gives 10,000 feet of ascent – the best day's mountaineering in Scotland.

The island of Rum, a few miles south of the Cuillin, takes a diamond shape 8 miles by 8. Its mainland side towers tall in half a dozen gabbro peaks, well seen from the Ardnamurchan or Morar coasts, while the Atlantic side is buttressed by 1000-foot sea-cliffs. The island's spell-binding power comes of its unmitigated wildness, conserved since 1957 by the Nature Conservancy Council. The basically poor land is largely given over to heather, deer, and wild goats.

The island of Mull to its south was like Skye a mainland peninsula until glaciers cut the sea-channel, and again like Skye was the site of a huge volcano from which lava flows piled up to many thousands of feet. The lava flows can be clearly seen as terraces along the west coast flanks. Just a mile off the south-west tip lies the minute but still more famous isle of Iona. It measures only 3 miles by 1 mile. Its rock is gneiss on the west coast, which is sculptured by sandy bays, and Torridonian sandstone across the brown moorlands eastward. It lies low to the sea, yet is given distinctive shape by the fort-like hill of Dun I (pron. Ee) at the north end. Close under the hill nestles Iona Abbey, built around 1200 by Ragnall, king of the Isles, on the site of Columba's original monastery. The stone is local granite ferried across the sound from the Ross of Mull.

St Columba came to Iona from Ireland in 563, and from this site converted the High-land Picts. His wooden monastery was later destroyed by Vikings, as also the first stone abbey built in the ninth century. In 1074 it was restored by Queen Margaret, and although that too fell to ruin, her chapel of St Oran has survived – Iona's earliest building. Its pink granite walls have a round-headed Norman doorway carved in pale sandstone. In the graveyard close beside the walls are buried 48 kings of Scotland (including MacBeth and Duncan), eight of Norway, and four of Ireland.

THE SOUTHERN HIGHLANDS

The Southern Highlands extend from the Isle of Arran on the Firth of Clyde to the south edge of Rannoch Moor. Arran is sheltered from the stormy west by the long arm of Kintyre peninsula. Its climate is mild, its rocks the most diverse in Scotland, hence its flora and landscape are peculiarly rich in variety. South of the Highland Line, which runs through its middle, are upland moors on sandstone; to its north are granite mountains rising on Goat Fell to 2866 feet. Sixteen peaks are linked to form two horse-shoes standing back to back with Cir Mhor at centre. Superb walking may be had along the crests, with green glens below and blue sea all around.

On the mainland, the dominating rock is mica-schist, which rises to 70 tops of 3000 feet or more, mostly rounded and grassy with craggy flanks. Great sea-lochs run far among the hills. The foothills around Loch Lomond and the Trossachs, and by the shores of Loch Awe and Loch Fyne, have frequently a more excellent combination of water, hill, and woodland than the more highly mountainous districts to the north.

The Trossachs are a group of 9 lochs and 20 hills east of Loch Lomond. Innumerable paths thread the district and circle the lochs, which are fringed by native hardwoods – oak, birch, ash, hazel, and holly – and by beech. The heart of the Trossachs is the wooded Achray Water, where it flows east from Loch Katrine.

Loch Lomond like the Trossachs owes its fame to the mountainous setting of native woodland around broad waters. The lochs's $4\frac{1}{2}$-mile breadth at the south end might have seemed too wide had variety not been given by a dozen islands. Eight miles up under Ben Lomond it narrows to half a mile, piercing 13 miles more into high hills. Glasgow is less than an hour away, hence there is abundant provision for water-sports. In summer, steamers ply on both Loch Lomond and Loch Katrine, allowing views superior to those from the shores.

After Ben Lomond, the most popular South Highland mountain is Ben Lawers, 3984 feet, on the north shore of Loch Tay. Arctic-alpine plants flourish on its many tops. The south slopes give excellent skiing, while the glen and river scenery round its base, especially in Glen Lyon and near Killin, rank with the Highlands' best.

CENTRAL HIGHLANDS

The Central Highlands extend from Rannoch Moor to the Great Glen. The landscape has a splendour of scale unknown to the Southern Highlands. Although of smaller area, it contains twice the number of high mountain tops. In shape they are massive humps like Ben Nevis or Ben Alder, yet closely packed and trenched deeply by glens like Glen Coe, Glen Etive, or Glen Nevis. Huge cliffs are often exposed on their north faces, and their hinterlands conceal much wilderness country.

One wilderness quite unconcealed is Rannoch Moor. It spreads out before you as soon as you top the Black Mount when heading north to Glen Coe. Between Clachlet on your left and Schichallion far eastward, it occupies 56 square miles, yet is so flat that the river draining east through a chain of lochs loses less than 100 feet in 10 miles. At the north-west end, the entrance to Glen Coe is dominated by the Buachaille Etive Mor, 3345 feet (the Great Herdsman of Etive). Shaped like a neolithic arrowhead, its rock-face is one of the most popular climbing centres in Scotland.

Three miles farther on, the river Coe plunges down a 3-mile gorge where the cliffs on either side rise to 3000 feet. The array of rock peaks on the left-hand side, split by ravines into the Three Sisters, is one of the wildest sights in Scotland. The glen meets the sea at Loch Leven, where the land suddenly opens out to give splendid vistas across Loch Linnhe to Ardgour. The coast of Lorn is graced by numerous medieval castles, but none is more beautifully sited among sea-lapped mountains than Castle Stalker, near Port Appin. Its rectangular tower, set on a tiny offshire islet, is still inhabited.

Loch Linnhe and the Firth of Lorn are the sea-flooded south half of the Great Glen, which splits Scotland north-east to the Moray Firth. Along this fault-line, the north block of Scotland has moved 65 miles south-west in relation to the south block. Earth tremors still occur.

At the head of Loch Linnhe, the Highlands rise to their highest point on Ben Nevis, 4406 feet. Shaped as a whale-back, it bears Britain's biggest cliff, 2 miles long and 2000 feet high, on its north-east flank. Other ranges like the Mamores and Grey Corries crowd it closely. Glen Nevis twists up between them all to give access to forty mountains. The waterfall of Steall in its upper part is 350 feet high.

CAIRNGORMS

The Cairngorms comprise 2200 square miles between the rivers Tay and Spey. At its heart lies the biggest group of high mountains in Scotland, a granite plateau of nearly 400 square miles. Four of its tops exceed 4000 feet and many others come close to that height. The forest and river landscapes fringing the district are unsurpassed in the Highlands. The gnarled Scots pines with bottlegreen tops and red bark are seen at their best at Rothiemurchus forest by Speyside, where they are often mixed with the lighter green of drooping birches, and in the forests of Mar and Ballochbuie at Deeside. These two approaches are quite different, for the Speyside forests stand on flat ground and the Deeside in glens. The Cairngorm plateaux high above them take no dramatic shapes – they are featureless wastes of stone in summer, of snow in winter – yet the huge scale on which the landforms are cast makes a deep appeal to everyone who walks there. The wide snowfields under still wider skies, the great corries plucked out of massive flanks, the long passes like the Lairig Ghru and Lairig an Laoigh, the very starkness of the land-scape, give a wilderness experience found nowhere else so fully. The development of

Speyside as a skiing centre has introduced thousands of people to that experience, while greatly diminishing it by weight of numbers on the northern slopes.

At Deeside, the main event of the year is the Braemar Gathering, held when the royal family are staying at Balmoral Castle in late summer. Vast acres of hillside are then purpled in heather. The gathering features Highland games and dancing, but the occasion is in reality more social than athletic.

WEST HIGHLANDS

The West Highlands include all land west of the Great Glen from Morven north to Loch Carron. No Highland scene could differ more from the flat-topped and spacious Cairngorms. At least 120 hills above 3000 feet are congregated to look on the map like a maze. They are steeper and more pointed than the south and central Highlands. The sea penetrates deeply up numerous glens close to the spine of the range, which draws heavy rainfall. Many of the sea-lochs are famous names – Carron, Duich, Alsh, Hourn, Nevis, and Sunart. The mountain maze is seen after study to be given order by long parallel glens running east to west; they give passes by road, track, and rail from the Great Glen to the coast: by Glen Garry to Loch Hourn, Glen Shiel to Loch Duich, Loch Arkaig to Morar, and Loch Eil to Mallaig. The romance of history has again made many of their names famous. All this land is deer forest and sheep-run, with crofting and forest work in the glens.

Fort William and Inverness at either end of the Great Glen are the best centres for exploring the region. The route from Fort William to the south-west peninsulas goes out to the head of Loch Eil (from which there is an excellent view back to Ben Nevis), then on to Ardgour, Morvern, Ardnamurchan, Moidart, and Morar. In all these districts the hills are relatively low with delightful coastal fringes, especially in Morar, where sands of pure white silica stretch 4 miles in coves and bays. Skerries close offshore give a good foreground to the Cuillin of Skye and Rum.

Moidart owes its beauty to water-filled glens framed by mountain ranges. Loch Shiel is the most famous of these, and not only because Prince Charles Edward Stewart raised his standard in 1745 at the loch's head at Glenfinnan. A monument has been raised to him there – a tall round tower on green fields. A stone highlander stands on top. The scene down Loch Shiel is still more renowned. The loch runs 17 miles south to Ardnamurchan within a mountain-frame of exquisite beauty. The broad nearer waters are greened by reflections from a wooded island, while the farther are given a double twist by mountain spurs thrusting into the loch and receding one behind the other into the distance.

From Glenfinnan northward the hill ranges mount in ever higher waves across Loch Arkaig, Glen Garry, and Glen Shiel to culminate in Glen Affric. Glens Garry and Shiel are gigantic troughs that split Scotland's spine from side to side. Glen Garry is much the

broader, and largely filled by Lochs Garry and Quoich (pronounced 'Kooich'). The former has a woodland scene rivalling that of Glen Affric, while Loch Quoich, spreading far out to the Knoydart hills, forms one of the most splendid of all Highland waterscapes – especially as seen from the new road to Skye, where that crosses north from the Garry over the hills to Cluanie.

Glen Shiel by comparison seems treeless and waterless, but instead is flanked by 20 mountains of dramatic landscape quality unrivalled by Garry. The narrow glen swoops down between them. The walls draw so close at one point as barely to leave room for both the road and the burn. The spear-shape of Faochaig (3000 feet) appears to block the glen's exit, until the road finally swings under the Five Sisters of Kintail to Loch Duich. The road to Skye winds along the north shore of Loch Duich to Kyle of Lochalsh. Near Dornie, it passes the thirteenth-century castle of Eilean Donan, which projects out of the sea close offshore. The site is idyllic, with the Cuillin of Skye filling the west horizon and the Five Sisters of Kintail rising behind.

THE NORTH-WEST HIGHLANDS

The pass across Scotland from Loch Carron to the Cromarty Firth is one of the most decisive Highland frontiers. To its north-west there occurs an abrupt change of rock and scene. The broad coastal strip of Wester Ross is built mainly of Torridonian sandstone as far as the Sutherland border at Assynt, and thereafter of Lewisian gneiss to Cape Wrath. These rocks give a poor soil in the glens and a lunar landscape on the hill-tops. In Wester Ross, especially by Loch Torridon and by Loch Maree in Gairloch, the glens are wooded; the mountains lift out of them in every shape from plum puddings to long swinging crests with arrowy towers. White quartzite often caps the summits, which on Beinn Eighe in Torridon can look like snow. North of Loch Maree, the land hardens; everywhere the rock crops out. The scene has an elemental wildness – rock and water set on bog. This culminates in Assynt, where sandstone mountains of monolithic shape project from a rolling moor of gneiss congested by many hundreds of lochs. As seen from the hills they light the land.

Ullapool, a fishing village on Loch Broom, is a good centre for exploring the coast, which is much less torn than the West Highlands'. Only Loch Broom and Loch Torridon make deep bites into the land. Among innumerable big bays, the most delectable is Gruinard. Several of its dozen coves have pink sand.

To enjoy the north coast near Cape Wrath, a move must be made to Durness. The outstanding features there are the quartzite mountains, which stand inland, and along the coast great grassy headlands buttressed by Britain's tallest mainland sea-cliffs. They are broken along their base by big caves where seals breed, sandy coves, sea-stacks, and natural arches.

The North-West Highlands embody much of Scotland's best landscape. Over all it is bare and windswept, yet the diversities are sudden, sharp, and inexhaustible. They are more readily seen than in other Highland regions, where they are no less numerous but not so obvious because widely spaced and hidden by hill ranges of greater scale and number. In all regions exploration brings a high reward, and never is that more true than when done on foot.

Holyrood House, Edinburgh

opposite Edinburgh Castle and National Gallery, Princes Street Gardens

opposite White Horse Close, Canongate, Edinburgh
overleaf The Forth Bridge

opposite St Andrew's, Fife: the harbour, with cathedral above

Crail, Fife

Lewis: Black houses at Valtos, Loch Roag

opposite Skye: crofting community

Isle of Arran: Cir Mhor and the
Castles from Goatfell

opposite Loch Awe, Argyll

Inveraray Castle, Loch Fyne,
Argyll

opposite Loch Lomond

opposite The Trossachs: Achray Water
flowing out of Loch Katrine

Clachlet, Rannoch Moor

The Buachaille Etive Mor, at the
entrance to Glen Coe

opposite The Head of Glen Coe, Argyll

Castle Stalker, Loch Linnhe,
Appin

opposite Ben Nevis, from the Great Glen

On the Crest of the Mamores,
with Glen Nevis below

The Cairngorms, from Loch
Morlich, above Speyside

Ben Eighe, Torridon, from Loch
Clair

ACKNOWLEDGMENTS

The Author and Publishers wish to thank the following for permission to reproduce the photographs appearing in this book:
Robert M. Adam for pages 15, 36, 40, 42, 52 and 58. The British Tourist Authority for page 19. J. Allan Cash for pages 61 and 62. Noel Habgood for pages 2, 9, 23, 24, 26-35, 37, 39, 43, 45, 47, 49, 51 and 63. A. F. Kersting for pages 11, 22, 38, 41, 44, 46, 48, 50, 53, 54-6 and 60. Kenneth Scowen for pages 6, 25, 57 and 59.
JACKET ILLUSTRATIONS
Front: Ben Nevis, seen from the Great Glen
Back: Edinburgh Castle, above the National Gallery and Princes Street Gardens
Both photographs were taken by the late Noel Habgood FRPS